FIRST LESSONS IN BACH FOR THE PIANO

Compiled and Fingered by WALTER CARROLL
Newly revised and edited by WILLAR~

CONTENTS

1. *MINUET:*
    A study in accent and in the correct timing of
    eighth-notes. 4

2. *MINUET:*
    A study in accent and in obtaining a proper balance
    of tone 6

3. *MINUET:*
    A study in the arpeggio of the common chord (close
    position) 8

4. *POLONAISE:*
    A study in phrasing and in the correct timing of
    sixteenth notes 10

5. *MARCH:*
    A study in syncopation and in keeping a steady beat
    throughout 11

6. *MINUET:*
    A study in contrasting rhythmic patterns between
    the hands. 13

7. *MINUET:*
    A study in legato playing, with careful balance of tone 14

8. *MINUET:*
    A study in tone-values, the lower part to be slightly
    more prominent than the upper 16

9. *MARCH:*
    A study in staccato touch, repeated notes and
    observance of rests 18

10. *MINUET:*
    A study in phrasing, legato touch and balance of tone 20

11. *MUSETTE:*
    A study in sustained notes and quality of tone 21

12. *BOURRÉE:*
    A study in contrasts of touch and independence of
    each hand 22

13. *MUSETTE:*
    A study in broken octaves and in neat phrasing. 24

14. *MINUET:*
    A study in expression, phrasing and beauty of tone 26

15. *GAVOTTE:*
    A study in phrasing, gradation of tone and
    cantabile playing 28

16. *MARCH:*
    A study in the accurate timing of triplets and in
    steadiness of rhythm 30

Cover art: Bach with His Family at Morning Devotion, *1870*
  by Toby Edward Rosenthal
  Archiv für Kunst und Geschichte, Berlin

Second Edition

The Bach Family
(From a painting by Toby E. Rosenthal)

ABOUT THIS NEW EDITION

Walter Carroll, a prominent English music educator, and a member of the faculty at the University of Manchester from 1893 to 1920, was especially active in the improvement of methods of teaching music to children. His *First Lessons in Bach,* used by thousands of teachers since the early part of this century, organized the easiest pieces either composed by Bach or used by his family in learning to play, with careful regard for musical content and pedagogical purposes. Through his efforts in this regard, Walter Carroll made these pieces, which he termed "charming, melodious, rhythmical, and of priceless value," more useful to teachers and more profitable for study.

Carroll selected most of this material (Nos. 1, 2, 3, 4, 5, 9, 10, 13, 14, and 16) from the well-known Notebook for Anna Magdalena Bach, which was presented by Bach to his second wife on her birthday in 1725. None of these pieces were composed by J.S. Bach. They were very probably compositions of the younger family members and friends or acquaintances. They were, nevertheless, family favorites, carefully copied into the book by Anna Magdalena or the children.

The remaining selections in the book comprise the simplest keyboard works by J.S. Bach himself. Nos. 6, 7, and 8 are from the *Suite in G Minor* BWV 822, composed during the Luneberg years, when Bach was yet a teen-ager. No. 11 is the *Musette* (in G major) from the 3rd *English Suite* (in G Minor), BWV 808, probably composed in Köthen in or before 1722. All of these original works were handed down through copies by students or family members, and there are no known manuscripts in Bach's own hand.

Since it is the present editor's policy to incorporate all the latest research into every Masterwork Edition, several corrections have been made here in an effort to make Carroll's presentation even more useful.

The original order of pieces as chosen by Carroll has been retained. The instructive comments have been slightly revised. Since Carroll was an Englishman, he used a few expressions not well-known to Americans. For example, more than one instructor might have been confused by his reference to eighth notes as "half-beats."

2

In Carroll's original presentation, almost all of the ornaments found in the opening selections were omitted, probably with a view to making these pieces more accessible to beginning students. We have restored them all, in footnotes, and they may be used or omitted at the teacher's discretion. By doing this, the present editor believes that the book will now be even more useful to a wider variety of students.

In several pieces, Carroll used the so-called "grace note" (♪) a small note with a cross-stroke. Such a note was NEVER used by Bach. In these cases, the correct ornament has been restored with explanatory footnotes.

In many Masterwork Editions, light gray print has been used to distinguish editorial phrasing, fingering, dynamics, tempo marks, and the like. In this case such a distinction is hardly necessary, since ALL of these markings are editorial. Carroll's own phrasing and other indications have been retained almost intact.

It should be emphasized that these markings are by Carroll, and NOT by J.S. Bach. In these selections Bach gave absolutely none of these indications.

Those who have used other editions of the same pieces by the present editor may wonder why the phrasing may be a bit different in this book than in those versions. Phrasing, dynamics and the like were left largely to the performer during Bach's day, and there are many acceptable ways to perform this music. Carroll's indications represent, in this editor's opinion, acceptable choices. Even the long phrases, indicating almost continuous legato, are in keeping with Bach's reference, in his introduction to the *Two and Three Part Inventions,* to the importance of developing a cantabile style of playing.

This new edition is more carefully engraved than the older ones. The music is more openly spaced for easier reading. These and many other improvements will be quickly noted and appreciated by any teacher who has used the older versions.

A FEW NOTES ABOUT ORNAMENTS

The ornaments used in this book are the *trill*, the *mordent*, the *appoggiatura*, and the *schleifer*. The basic rules for playing the ornaments are outlined below:

All of Bach's ornaments begin on the beat of the main (full-sized) note and take their time value away from the main note.

- The *trill*, indicated by ᴧ or *tr* , begins on the upper auxiliary (next higher scale tone). It must have at least four notes but may have as many as the tempo of the piece and the value of the note will allow.

The trill may end with an anticipation of the following note, or with a termination consisting of two notes (the lower auxiliary and the main note), which are played at the same speed as the trill.

- The *mordent* (ᴧᴧ) is a "biting" ornament. The main note is quickly alternated with its lower auxiliary.

- The *appoggiaturas* (♪) which appear in this book are indicated by small eighth notes. These are long appoggiaturas. They recieve half the value of the following note. (If the following note is a dotted note, the appoggiatura generally receives 2/3 the value. In some cases they sound better when given only 1/3 the value of the dotted note.) Appoggiaturas should be accented and the main note played more softly.

- The *schleifer* ᴧᴧ is a "sliding" ornament, usually used to fill in the gap between a note and the previous one. An example of its correct performance is shown on page 20, in the 6th measure.

In Bach's day, ornaments were freely added to the music by the performer when a section of music was repeated, according to the following rules:

- Trills or upper appoggiaturas were most often added when the music descended (by step or by leap).

- Mordents were added when the music ascended (by step or by leap).

- Lower appoggiaturas were added when the music ascended by step only.

- Schleifers were generally added when the music ascended by leap.

Willard A. Palmer, Editor

1. Minuet

A study in accent and in the correct timing of eighth-notes.

(a) The original manuscript shows a *mordent* (ᰯ) over each of these notes. Alternate the written note with the note a 2nd below very quickly, on the beat, for example:

(b) The "grace note" (♪) with cross-stroke given by Carroll is in error. The autograph shows no cross-stroke, and the ornament is a long appoggiatura.

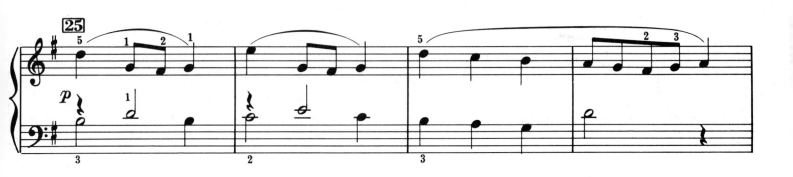

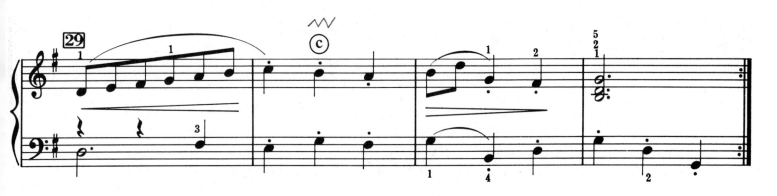

ⓒ Here the manuscript shows a trill (⚡). It may be played: 𝄞

2. Minuet

A study in accent and in obtaining a proper balance of tone.

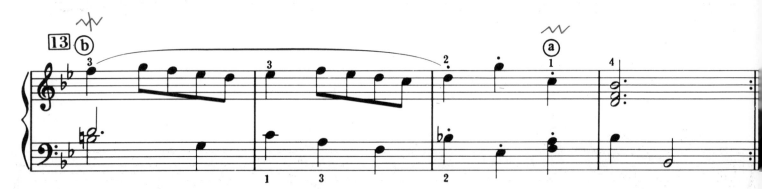

ⓐ The original manuscript shows a *trill* (𝄌) over each of these notes. They should begin on the note above the written note, and need not have many repercussions. For example, the first one may be played: or

ⓑ Here the original manuscript has a *mordent* (𝄌). Alternate the written note with the note a 2nd below very quickly, on the beat:

At the close of this movement the previous Minuet may be repeated.

3. Minuet

A study in the arpeggio of the Common Chord (close position).

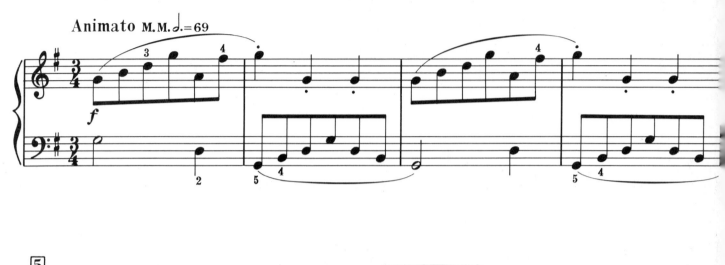

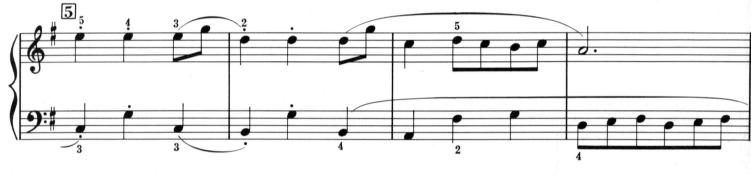

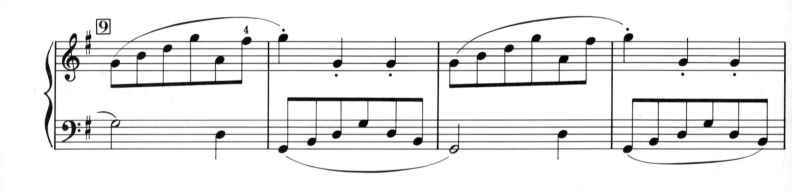

4. Polonaise

A study in phrasing and in the correct timing of sixteenth-notes.

At the close of this movement Minuet No. 3 may be repeated.

5. March[ⓐ]

A study in syncopation and in keeping a steady beat throughout.

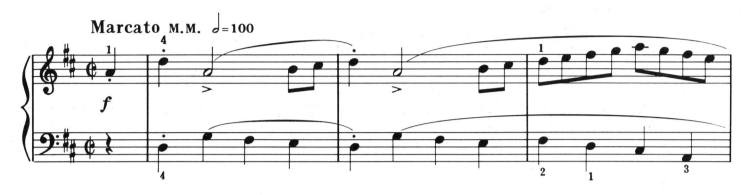

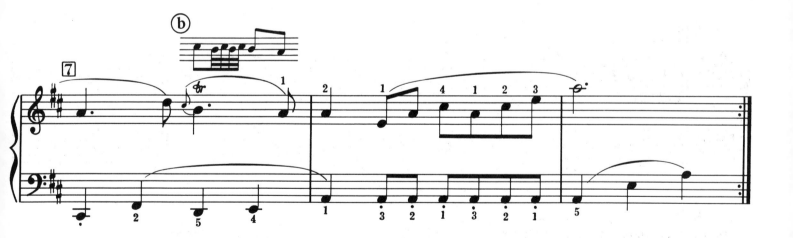

ⓐ This piece is now believed to have been composed by one of J.S. Bach's sons, Carl Philip Emanuel Bach, at the age of 14.

ⓑ The "grace note" (𝅗𝅥) with cross-stroke given by Carroll is incorrect. The text here is corrected to agree with the original manuscript.

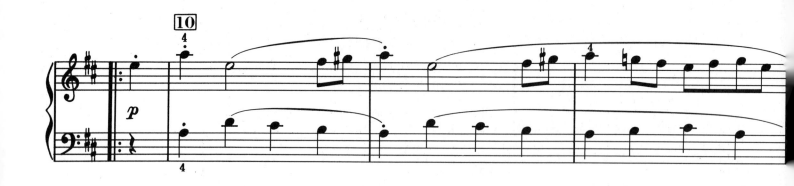

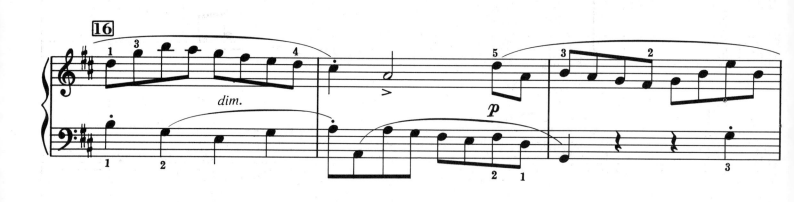

6. Minuet

A study in contrasting rhythmic patterns between the hands.

Nos. 6, 7, 8, after being studied separately, may be grouped together for performance in the order 7, 6, 8.

7. Minuet

A study in legato playing, with careful balance of tone.

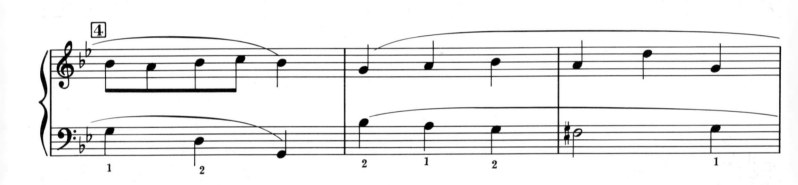

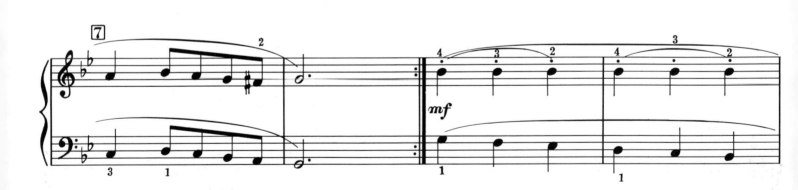

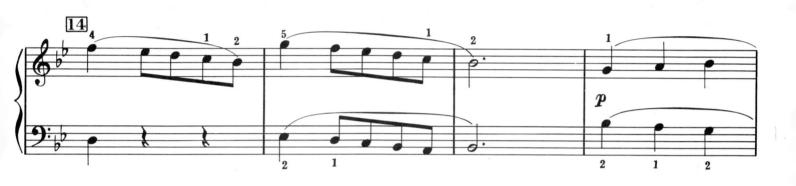

8. Minuet

A study in tone - values, the lower part to be slightly more prominent than the upper. (Compare with No. 7)

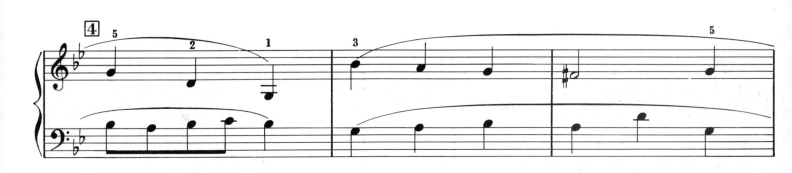

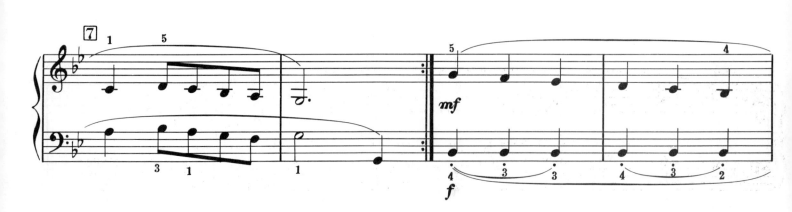

9. March

A study in staccato touch, repeated notes and observance of rests.

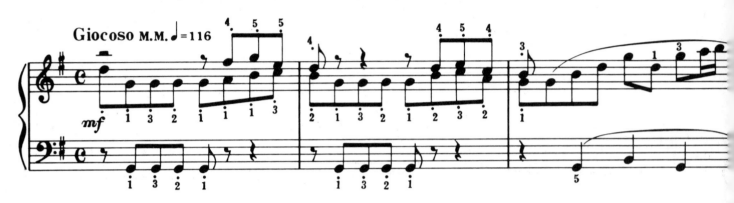

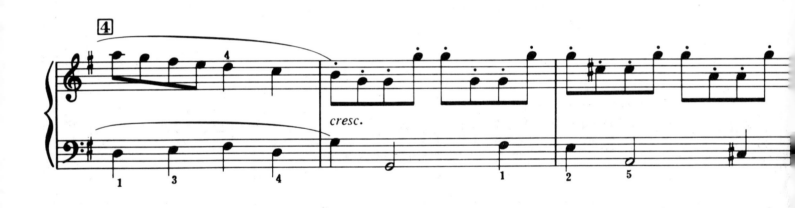

(a) The manuscript has [musical notation] This may be played as shown in Carroll's text, or as follows: [musical notation]

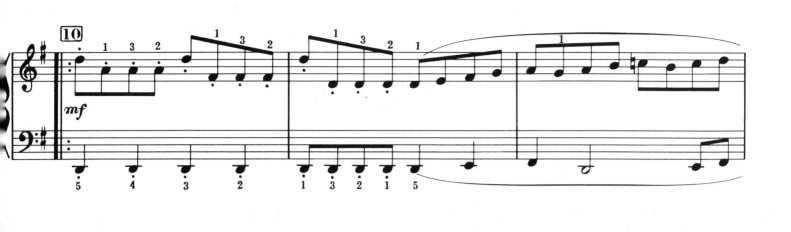

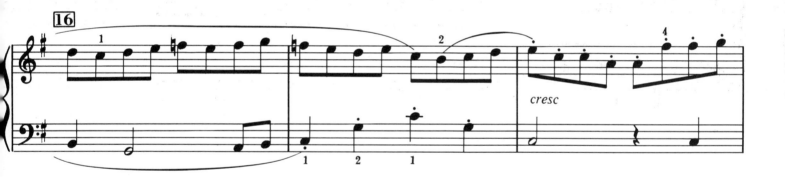

10. Minuet

A study in phrasing, legato touch and balance of tone.

ⓐ The ''grace note'' (♪) given by Carroll is incorrect. The original manuscript has a SCHLEIFER (᷇), which is played as shown in the small staff above the ornament, in our text.

11. Musette

A study in sustained notes and quality of tone.

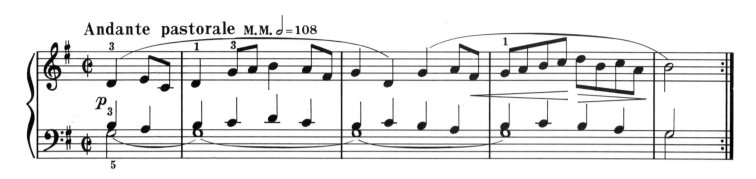

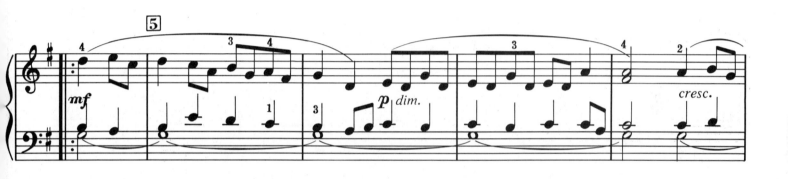

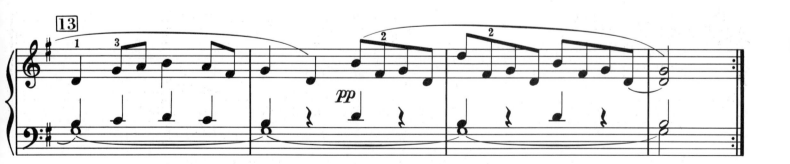

12. Bourrée

A study in contrasts of touch and independence of each hand.

ⓐ Carrol gives the tempo as *Vivace* M.M. = 108. To this editor, this seems excessively fast.

13. Musette

A study in broken octaves and in neat phrasing.

14. Minuet

A study in expression, phrasing and beauty of tone.

Larghetto e sostenuto M.M. ♩= 96

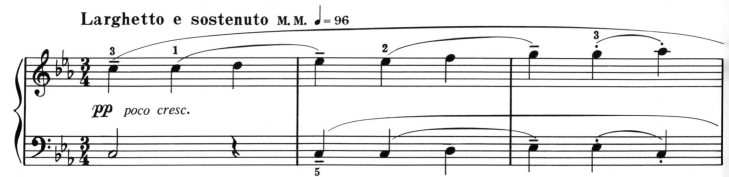

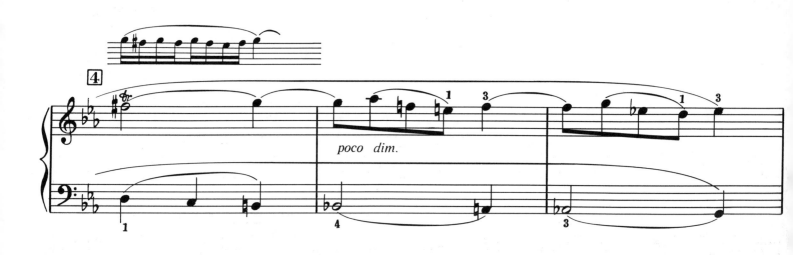

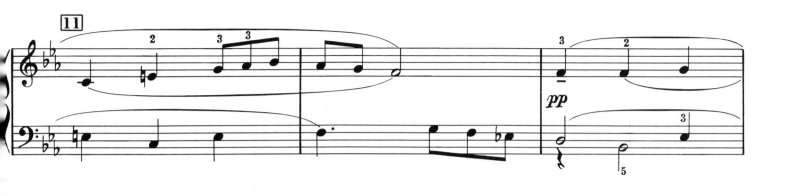

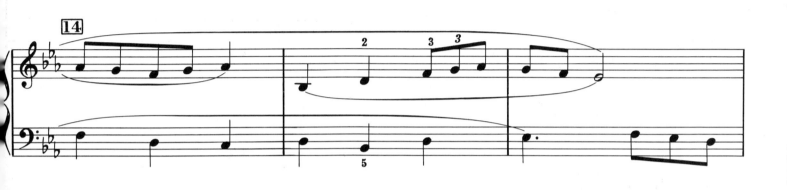

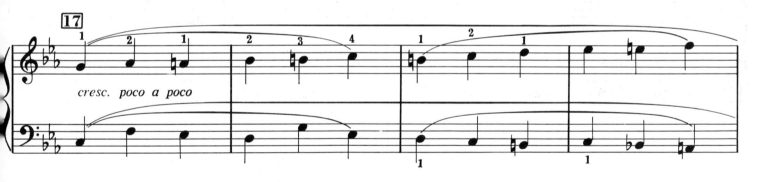

27

15. Gavotte

A study in phrasing, gradation of tone and cantabile playing.

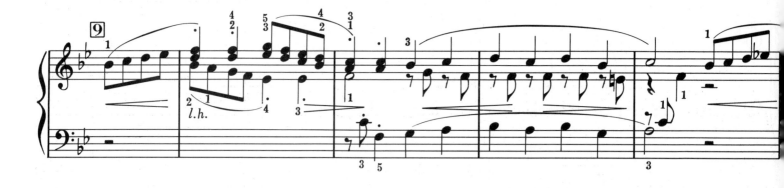

D.C. al Fine

16. March

A study in the accurate timing of triplets and in steadiness of rhythm.

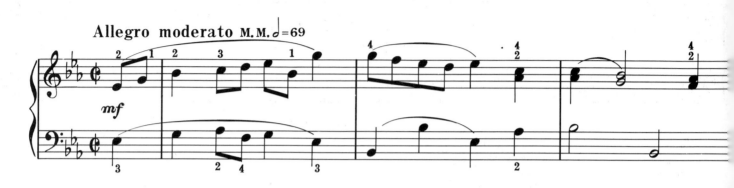